# NEW & SELECTED POTATOES

**John Hegley** was born in Newington Green, London, in 1953, and grew up in Luton and Bristol. After attending Bradford University he returned to London and joined the community arts collective Interaction; he has continued their interactive ethos ever since. During the early 1980s he was a regular performer at London's Comedy Store and also recorded with The Popticians, including two sessions for John Peel's BBC Radio One programme. He has worked regularly on radio and television and remains a popular performer across the UK and abroad, blending poetry, comedy and song. In 2012 he was the Writer in Residence at Keats House, in Hampstead, London. His *New & Selected Potatoes* (Bloodaxe Books, 2013) spans a thirty-year publishing career, drawing together new poems with selections from twelve previous collections.

# JOHN HEGLEY

# NEW & SELECTED
# POTATOES

## EDITED BY ANDY CHING

BLOODAXE BOOKS

ISBN: 978 1 85224 978 6

First published 2013 by
Bloodaxe Books Ltd,
Highgreen,
Tarset,
Northumberland NE48 1RP.

www.bloodaxebooks.com
For further information about Bloodaxe titles
please visit our website or write to
the above address for a catalogue.

Supported by
**ARTS COUNCIL
ENGLAND**

Cover design: Neil Astley & Pamela Robertson-Pearce.

Printed in Great Britain by Bell & Bain Limited, Glasgow, Scotland, on
acid-free paper sourced from mills with FSC chain of custody certification.

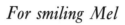

*For smiling Mel*

# ACKNOWLEDGEMENTS

Acknowledgements are due to the editors and publishers of the books in which many of these poems first appeared. The poems 'Grandad's Glasses' and 'Max' first appeared in *Visions of the Bone Idol* (Little Bird Press, 1984) but were later republished in *Glad to Wear Glasses* (André Deutsch, 1990) and *My Dog is a Carrot* (Walker Books, 2002). The poem 'Wentworth Place, Hampstead... (Dear John, age sixteen)' was published in the Keats House anthology, *Here We Go Round the Mulberry Tree* (2012), while 'The Differences between Dogs and Deckchairs' is published simultaneously in *I Am a Poetato: An A-Z of Poems about People, Pets and Other Creatures* (Francis Lincoln Children's Books, 2013). The collections *The Brother-in-Law and Other Animals* (Down the Publishing Company, 1986), *Can I Come Down Now, Dad?* (Methuen, 1991) and *These Were Your Father's* (Methuen, 1994) were later republished in *The Family Pack* (Methuen, 1997). The collections *Five Sugars Please* (1993), *Love Cuts* (1995), *Beyond Our Kennel* (1998), *Dog* (2000), *The Sound of Paint Drying* (2003) and *Uncut Confetti* (2006) were published by Methuen; *The Adventures of Monsieur Robinet* (2009) by Donut Press; and *Peace, Love & Potatoes* (2012) by Serpent's Tail, to whom particular thanks are due.

Rights to reprint poems from this book are controlled by Methuen and Serpent's Tail for their volumes, and by the author via United Agents for other poems.

# CONTENTS

# New Potatoes

(2013)

# A Lean Towards the Light

Mister William Wordsworth won't take sugar in his porridge.
He takes honey.
It's not to do with the money
or the flavour
as much as the moral objection
to the method of production.
Mister William Wordsworth measures out his conscience
with his spoon.
In the face of what is taking place,
the boon of Mister Wordsworth's gesture may seem slight, but
   it's a lean towards the light.

When I put my recycling out
I know my contribution's
not equivalent to manning of the barricades in nineteen-thirties Spain
but, again,
   it's a lean towards the light –
a step in the direction
that seems right.

Like a monocotyledon that's broken through the surface,
starting its existence as a blade of grass
or daffodil,
   the move that's phototropic
   might be only microscopic,
but it's a lean, instinctive in the little bean,
   it's a lean towards the light.

## Tiger Meditation

Embrace...the tiger
is a move in t'ai chi.
Chi is a word
for the invisible blood
which is not blood,
which flows through the body.
T'ai chi is a way of staying sprightly
with small exercise,
like a household cat stays ready to pounce
with what seems like simple stretches.
In those stretches flows the chi.
Yawn like you mean it.
Yawn for all that is.
Yawn for your lawnmower
if you have one,
if you have to,
but put your hand in front of your mouth.
Remember you are not a tiger
and you are not paying enough attention.

## And Did Those Feet

I am sitting beside the till in the Picasso Café, Chelsea,
and standing right beside me,
about to pay his bill, is George Best.

Wanting to look, but not to stare,
I notice first his trousers, with lots of pockets,
and then his feet.
George Best's feet.
Surprisingly small.
Twinkle twinkle, little toes.
George Best's feet. Wow!
If only I could give this page to him now.
Make a ball of it.
Screw up this page and roll it by him.
And see George Best dribbling
with my scribbling.

# London, 2012

Backing and advancing.
Competing and dancing.
Outside the Olympic centre
my brother who was once a fencer
and Sally, from the north,
who was one also.
They have taken up plastic swords
from a stall provided to catch
the enthusiasm of children
and perhaps set them on a path
of lunge and parry.
Marcel and Sally
in touch with their own younger selves.
A brief exhibition of joy.
Harking back.
Sallying forth.

# A Sign of the TV Times

Our TV, back in the heyday,
was from the people of Rentaset.
You see, we didn't need to *own* a set,
we just needed to own the joy of our programmes.
And of course there was something so glowing about knowing
that when the repairman came
you were not bogged down by the baggage of payment activities.
It was already sorted and you could happily exchange
the tokens of a truly human commerce.

As I recollect, there was never a repairwoman,
but how welcome she'd have been,
laying out the toolkit that was all part of the deal,
sucking on her boiled sweet in her blue boilersuit,
badge stitched onto her breast pocket,
mind switched on to your home-loving hearts
and needs,
not sucking you dry, not with the feel of a breakdown leech,
and if your set was beyond the pale or the bucket
then you knew replacement would be both speedy
and free.
And once more you could sit back – back, picking up the threads
of young Ned Sherrin's production
of *That Was The Week That Was*,
even though the priest had told you
that in terms of good Roman Catholic viewing
you were better off watching *Bonanza*.

I like to think of Father Bustin, inside the sanctuary of his priest's
home,
with a Rentaset.
Like faith,
something
you couldn't buy.

# The Golfing Girlfriends

At the First Hole
  She felt sure she saw a razorbill cutting a dash.

At the Second
  She reckoned it may have been a straggler, storm-blown inland.

At the Third Hole
  She consults a fellow putter, who says the bird was probably a
  guillemot.

At the Fourth Hole
  She notes how strolling the course has an ever-increasing toll on
  her knee joints.

At Hole Five
  She hit her best drive of the round, by quite a distance.

At the Sixth Hole
  She wonders again where is her friend Daisy.

At the Seventh Hole
  She digs up quite a divot in spite of her pivotal success.

At Hole Eight
  She inwardly announces *There's late and there's ludicrous, dear Daisy.*

At the Ninth
  She gives herself some praising for a fine line of projection.

At Hole Ten
  In a pressing rainburst she presses her umbrella for protection.

At the Eleven Hole
  She thinks *Why* is *a golf umbrella so enormous?*

At Hole Twelve
    She delves into her packetful of sweet Rhubarb and Custards.

At the Thirteenth Hole
    She thinks *So come on, lazy Daisy. Where are you?*

At the Fourteenth
    Daisy joins her, with clubs and explanation.

At the Fifteenth
    The hole in Daisy's world is something larger than The Fifteenth.

At the Sixteenth
    She is sharing out her sweeties with her friend in this distraction.

At the Seventeenth
    And she thinks, *Hold on, a guillemot's no more likely than a razorbill, flying inland. What was he on about?*

At the Eighteenth Hole
    Daisy wonders if they have golfing greens in Greenland. Or Iceland.

## The Differences between Dogs and Deckchairs

A deckchair doesn't beg
or cock up its leg.
Deckchairs don't sniff each other.
Deckchairs can't swallow,
or swim or growl.
Deckchairs aren't her or him.
Deckchairs don't join in games with sticks.
There are no prizes for well-trained deckchairs.
Deckchairs rarely have names, except 'deckchair'.

People don't have trouble putting up a dog.
Dogs' legs don't have little notches in.
A deckchair's legs are much stiffer with no knees.
A dog is better at running after Frisbees.
Deckchairs can be stacked quite neatly.
Dogs have more hairs.
Deckchairs have more letters.
Deckchairs don't sniff about in autumn leaves.
A deckchair receives little praise.

# Bats

D.H. Lawrence
shared abhorrence,
beleaguered by those bats;

though I sense that what he showed us, at that
eavesdropping of bats,
did not reveal his full feeling for the bat.

While he didn't seem that happy with the flit of happy bats –
in his hair and overwear, disturbing air, giving D.H. Lawrence
more than his fair share of getting-up-and-at-you bats –

despite all his drats and scary scats for scattering those bats, it's
not the total picture. I bet that there were other bits,
yes, I would add a *gladness* in his Nibs who came from Notts.

He would not have *done without* those flappy, batty bots,
but like a mum and dad who let steam blow off their lids,
there's steam above but love below, that they don't show their kids.

21

# Dear Mister D.H. Lawrence

I am a former pupil of yours.
I hope this letter reaches you,
like you used to reach us boys
        when you were teaching us in Croydon.

Your country's turned its back on you,
turned your paintings round so they just
                stare at the gallery wall:
                unfit for consumption,
                        admiration.
                We just admire their gall.

You have been hurt by England
    but to me you're still 'Sir';
    though your temper was short
                and you told us when you taught us
                that we were nothing but a shower.
Still, you brought out our so reticent rainbows,
and I'm writing, Sir,
                to register my support.

# Fanny's Song

I'm Fanny Brawne,
forlorn for him who set me all a-dazzle:
all my drizzle, all my sun,
out of sight
but not of mindfulness.
Our young and fledgling flight,
all his verse and all his horseplay,
all my wheelbarrow of light.
Beside the distant Spanish Steps
and shortly set to vanish,
with companions stood around his head, so grim,
he spoke to them be-calmingly,
told them, 'Do not be alarmed.'
Ever assistant,
his bedside manner did not desert him.

## Grandad's Losing Grandma Song

We were married, blessed and blazing,
my blancmange.
Your fondness I kept as a token of sweetness.
The lion that you had awoken
would prowl a hunger,
but anger was pointless –
there are times when it's best
that the worst is accepted.
I landed your hand in marriage
but your feet had ideas of their own.

¶

Dear John, age sixteen,

It's going to be hard leaving the old town. You are going to leave your mates, you are going to leave your football team, you are going to leave your brother, you are going to leave your lack of belief in your abilities. Do you know what these are, John? There was a time when you might have called them your gifts from God. You might yet call them such again. Some of these gifts are, of course, gifts possessed by many: the smell of sage, the sight of the delicacy of stamens, the feeling of the sun upon your spectacles. Others are gifts more rare: the ability to make people laugh, the ability to make people dance and the ability to make people sick. We all have our failings. The recognition of your own will help with your acceptance of the shortcomings of others.

All the best, Sub,
up the Hatters,

John, age fifty-eight

## A Short Testament of Will

I Will that the youngster with the talent in the neglected seam will be found out.

I Will that the child like myself, whose voice was with song but was unheard, shall be heard.

I Will that those in the place where the teachers have not the wherewithal to call forth the golden voice in the darkness of schooldays shall be assisted in finding the gems that lie hidden.

I Will that experts in the act of digging shall go forth to the un-dug places and bring out the singing souls.

I Will that the spilling of the untold talent be fostered and nurtured and celebrated.

I Will that those who are thus brought forth before us to assist in our advancement be assisted in the management of their genius.

In the meantime I will attempt to give a hand in the steering of these matters.

John Hegley, 2nd April 2013

FROM

# Peace, Love & Potatoes

(2012)

## An Alien Address

Do you have bendy buses
or are you jet-propelled?
Do you have those things on tube trains,
to be held onto when it's crowded,
I don't know what they're called?
How much is there in your world
that you haven't got a name for?
Do you ever get appalled
when your brand new central heating
has been shoddily installed
by a bunch of cowboys?
Are you green, are you translucent,
do you have any pets?
Do you have mental illness
or menthol cigarettes?
Do you ever feel you don't fit in with all the rest?
Do you feel like an outsider,
like a money spider in a nest
of penniless termites?
Do you ever say 'to be honest'?
Do you ever say 'for my sins'?
Or are truthfulness and repentance where
another world begins?
Do your bins get emptied on a Tuesday?
Do you have three-legged races
you can compete in on your own?
Do you have stripy deckchairs that get wind-blown
when they're vacant?
Is there anybody out there?
Have you got ears for this?
Have you got liver tablets
or the equivalent of Bristol?
Do you wear a pair of glasses, for maybe you have eyes?
Do you start off as a baby and then increase in size
but lose your sense of wonderment in the process?

Do you ever get on a crowded train
and have to put your luggage in the vestibule,
and do you ever sit in the seat nearest the door
so you can keep an eye on it
and then more people get on
and you have to stand up and say
'Excuse me, but could you move out of the way, please,
I cannot see my luggage'?

## Being Is Believing

I believe in you.
I believe in you
being close to me.
I believe in you being close to me
intimately.
I believe in you being close to me
intimately, regularly.
I believe in you being close to me
intimately, regularly,
just not today.
I believe in you being close to me
intimately, regularly
just not today
because sometimes
I need to be with myself alone
all the better to be with you
more intimately.

## Let Us Play

Let's dig tunnels.
Let's build bridges.
Let's get close
like clouds of midges.
What was under
Mr Brunel's hat?
His love letters
and his sand*widges*.
Let us cross that big divide.
Let us go and coincide.
And with the space between deducted,
let us mind what's been constructed.

You provide the motion and I'll start the debate.
You provide the provender and I'll supply the napkin and the plate.
Let's combine this life of mine with your own slender fate.
Let me elaborate.
Let's be thick as thieves can be.
Let's thicken up the ice and then entice the world to skate.
You be narrow, I'll be straight.
You be weight and I'll be volume.
Let's make a pair of zeroes
make a bigger figure eight.
Let's collaborate.

# Quackers

When we first moved from London, my father kept on his job in the capital. He would make his way each evening from High Holborn to St Pancras and then onwards by steam train, back to family and foodstuff.

He goes his way home through the early winter city, stopping to do brief business with a street vendor at a novelty stall displaying a colourful variety of plastic frivolities. It's nearing Christmas. He'll get something for the youngsters. Some small, near-Christmas knick-knacks. The plastic ducks look good. The vendor demonstrates that they are whistles. Doubly good, then. Heading for the terminus, the train and the *Evening News*, and the eventual warm embrace and nibble of a kiss.

Back in the home, my mother is well pleased with the bird presentation. My younger sister holds one and I the other. My older brother is above this brittle birdlife. Angela and I blow into the mouthpieces at the same moment. The bottom beak of each bird drops in slow response and the quacking comes comically forth. 'They'll look nice on the tree,' Mum advises. Thread is found, along with their new hanging positions.

And henceforth they come out annually to beduck the pineful foliage. The whistling ducks, ornamental now, are whistling ducks no longer. Seen. Not heard.

But there are worse endings at Christmas for a bird.

# Extravagance

When I was a boy,
extravagantly was not the way
things were done in our home.
Budgets and belts were tight.
Christmas, we pushed out the boat,
but measuredly:
one box of dates,
one packet of figs,
one bottle each of sherry and port.
As much as could be afforded.
And the lifting smoke of my father's cigar
was the star prize.
The smoke, he blew it upwards in a ring.
And he sat back with the comfort of a King
Edward.

# Taking Out the 'in it' and Putting 'innit' In It

This clock has still got a lot of mileage in it.
This clock is well-stocked with mileage, innit.

This society has still got deep class divisions in it.
Class wise, this society is still deeply divided, innit.

This potato has the possibility of the most delightful bloom in it.
This potato is bloomful of possible delight, innit.

This gap between the floorboards has got some little bits of old
   cheese in it.
Have you thought about doing some hoovering, innit.

# A Show for My Sister

When the cardboard curtain
came up to show
my first puppet performance,
it was for you and you only,
my space-hopping poppet.
You, in our living room,
giving room to the scissor-snipped crew
shipped in from Woolworths for a shilling.
My cut-out cast were not cut out
for anyone but you,
Angie Boo.
You, my key and only witness.
How willingly you paid your heed
and your entrance monies.
How eager your attention
as each figure drew forth
the cutlass of its character
and spilled the beans of what it had to do.
What an audience you were, until you began fidgeting
in Act Twelve, Scene Two.

# Keep Your Receipts, Mister Keats

*A song composed whilst researching John Keats with an imminent visit
to The Marine Theatre in Lyme, home of local heroine Mary Annin,
famous for her fossil-hunting*


I'm going to Lyme Regis. Is it Dorset? Is it Devon? Soon I'll know.
I've been told there was a fossil-finding woman of Lyme Regis, long ago.
She sold her finds as curios.
She sounds to be somebody most intriguing
but my curiosity's directed elsewhere at the mo'.
I've been going through the poetry and letters
of a man who didn't have sufficient time.
A man who walked on Hampstead Heath in autumn
with his vessel full of Mister William Shakespeare and the fruitfulness of
    rhyme.

John Keats, with your days laid out so meagre,
it's no surprise
how eager was your pace.
John Keats, you stuffed your notebook rather than your ego and your face.
John Keats, wild about Will Shakespeare,
but I'm not sure if you'd heard of William Blake.

John Keats, your muse was both a marvel and, in terms of making money,
    your mistake.
John Keats, you sat outside on coaches,
it encroached upon your health,
your wealth did not provide the funds
for you to settle in the dry
you'd have preferred.
John Keats, you did the doctor's training
but decided you were cut out for the word.

The first I heard you mentioned was in a Loudon Wainwright song,
then in another one by Morrissey.
I didn't know your legacy
but still I sang along.

I've been going through the poetry and letters
of a man who later than his life
was so much better known.
A man whose pay day came too late for him to get a ticket
to get sat inside the coach
instead of getting wet and windblown.
Up beside the driver,
a man who was no skiver.
But the world it can deprive a
man, no matter what his feats.
Can I lend you a fiver, please?
No, make that a tenner, Sweet
John Keats.

John Keats, you wanted to complete
a life that was held completely in the grip of poetry,
because poetry you held to be most naturally holy.
John Keats, you suggested that a poem should come out complete,
as certain and as surely as a leaf upon a tree,
but preferably
not as slowly.

Did you used to walk the dog?
Did you have a dialogue?
While the dog did what it had to do,
did you share a verse or two?
And were they the doggy's treats,
John Keats?

¶

Dear John Keats,

Last Thursday I was round your house in Hampstead where I bought a book of letters you had written in the early nineteen-hundreds. I was with Celia. It was really a lovely afternoon and we took tea on your veranda, on the bench.

And slugging on that mug of tea,
it would be unknown to me
that in my bag and in your book,
there you are, John, slagging off the French manner of speaking.
It's my father's native country.
It's my father's mother lingo!
You went into your tool bag and you went in with a spanner and
    a cheeky monkey wrench,
when you were slagging off the language of the French.
Is 'slagging off' a turn of phrase you know, John?
Do you like DIY or Dan Defoe, John?
I'd like to meet you some time and have a good old natter.
Do you use powder on your teeth, are you a hatter on The Heath?
John, you may be miles away,
in spite of which I'd like to say

John, *je suis si enchanté*,
'scuse my French

P.S. It's some days later and I realise it's not just the French, is it, John? No, you're not too keen on the people of Devon, either. One letter says the Battle of Waterloo would have been lost were all Englishmen Devonians. And then the Scots, you say they are comparatively clean but they never laugh. I told this to a Scottish friend, who said 'That made me laugh, but then I've got some Irish in me.' Let's not go into what you say about the Irish!

# A.J. Curtis and the Fish

I walk with Tony.
Moonshine big, a bright and Brighton button overhead.
We tread the homeward esplanade.
The scaly plateful those unruly waves have laid before us
is now tight in Tony's wide
and grateful grasp:
this tossed marine inhabitant,
windfallen fruit of the sea.

Three years before, the world had thrown up Tony.
It was back in Bristol. We, the energetic students,
set about the brightening of our gloomy sixth form common room.

Tony, in the year below me, was unknown to me.
He had dipped his bare feet in the paint bucket.
And we held him bodily, topside down,
and he walked the planks of strutted ceiling,
making all his markings there
and mightier impression on me.

My mate to be: in a world of pranks and disappointments,
an artist.
And now,
here he is beside this sea, with the gift of fish
in his fingers.

Just for a chuckle, Tony once hurled his crash helmet,
arcing it into the surging waters of Vassals Park.

And now, out of the dark, the world has thrown him back
a mackerel.

# Peace, Love and Potatoes

Wed in 1944,
my mother
kept on peeling from the pick
of the potato sack,
with the occasional knack
of getting their jackets off
all in one piece.
Quite a trick. A quiet feat.
Like her and dad's feeling for each other:
uninterruptedly alive
and complete.

¶

My dear grandchild,

Here in Nice it is a beautiful morning. Carnival time has come round. Another winter so quick on the heels of the last. My friend Mireille and I have been swimming in the sea, which buoys up the old body as readily as the young.

Your aunt Daisy and I have made our carnival masks from papier-mâché. They are next to the fire, drying on the dog. Daisy has just asked me to place some of the carnival confetti she has cut up into the envelope, so you can share the spirit of the carnival when you throw it over your own dog.

I sit here with the windows and shutters open. Yes, here in Nice it is a beautiful morning and yet I am desolate to hear of your terrible experience at the school. Please make sure I've got the sequence of events correct, because I am making correspondence on your behalf.

So, you joined the Scottish country dancing class in your lunch break. It was your first time and it had taken courage to go along because some foolish boys see dancing as an activity to be ashamed of. After a while in the class you nervously laughed out loud because, for the first time, your feet were learning, learning the wonders of making dance steps. Intimidated by your laughter, the teacher ordered you out of the room, accusing you of play-acting and buffoonery.

This is the story as I understand it. Please hand the enclosed letter to the woman, along with the photograph of myself on stage with the most famous dancing company in all of France. I want her to realise the calibre of dancing stock with which she is toying. As a dancer in Paris I would kick my legs and laugh, laugh. Laugh at the filth who came to ogle us from the pit. Except your grandfather, of course.

Your grandmother

¶

Dear Mister Pickwick,

I've been reading your papers and am enjoying your capering very much. I obtained my green volume of these adventures from my local public library lending department. I feel sure that your creator, Mister C. Dickens, would have approved of such places – particularly because of the benefit to readers unable to afford a text of their own. I have renewed the book four times and paid about seventy pence in fines, but you are worth it. Seventy pence is fourteen shillings in your money. There have been many changes since your day; far fewer people wear hats, for instance. Also, in your day did you have, I wonder, to pull your luggage along? You're always travelling about, aren't you? Today I read aloud a passage from one of your travels to some blue-clad school children in Northumberland – the story where you mistakenly settled in the twin room of a hotel in Ipswich, which was actually the accommodation of an unsuspecting woman. There you were, in your nightcap, behind the curtain of the bed, ready for sleeping when in she comes and starts her preparations for dreaming, not dreaming that you are in the immediate vicinity. I asked the youngsters to relate the tale in verse and one of them put: 'Mister Pickwick went to bed, with his nightcap on his head.' (Yes, you even wore hats to sleep in in your day.) And someone else called Shannon wrote, 'Mr Pickwick in his nightcap, watching the woman take off her slap.' Yes, Mister Pickwick, you can be gratified in knowing that the youth of another millennium are engaged by your appearance, your ambience and your antics. Here is a drawing for you to complete.

Your admirer

# At a Public Reading by an English Hero

Tell us about Copperfield and Oliver
and his wishing for the dishing out of more.
Let's hear about the optimist Micawber,
his persistent hopes of what lay up afore.
Do divulge of Mister Scrooge and poor Miss Havisham,
that disenchanted woman who set all her world alight.
Tell us any of your stories that you fancy
but please don't tell us Nancy's tale tonight.

Let your prose expose those social conditions
where there should be an improvement of the plight.
Tell us and impel us to correction,
to protection and to setting things aright.
Perhaps pick one of Mister Pickwick's Papers,
Dingley Dell at Christmastime would do us very well,
but please don't tell us Nancy's tale tonight.

Don't spill the beans of her and Bill.
Don't put your public through the mill.
Mr Dickens, as you will,
yes, as you fancy up until
that villainous and sinking bag of spite.
Let common sympathy prevail,
leave us hearty, leave us hale,
and please don't tell us Nancy's tale tonight.

## Sooty (or The Bird Who Reminded Me
## of My French Grandma)

It must have come sweeping down the bungalow chimney
when the fire was off duty,
that feathery black beauty
that was never going to back up the smokestack.
Was it a crow?
Was it a raven?
Or was it a very sooty pigeon?
We didn't know.
We just knew that whatever it was,
it didn't want to go.
For all our shuffling and shooing,
nothing doing, going-wise.
That ruffled kerfuffle
flitting around the sitting room,
eventually sitting down at rest
on the central light fitting.
Eyeing us.
Contemplating starting up a nest, perhaps.
So I run to the bungalow's rear,
splaying open the French windows.
The bird follows and flies,
steering away through the stretched gap,
going back to its element.
And my mum begins to clap
that ruffled kerfuffle,
that disorderly duster,
that freaky beaky bungalow invader
that got us in a right flap.

¶

My dear grandchild,

Thank you for the drawing of your dog, which is accurate but lacking in vitality. I can see that the creature is asleep, like our own, here beside the fire. It is a challenge to breathe life into the image. A challenge to which you have failed to rise. If I did not tell you such things I would be shirking my work as a grandmother.

So, you wish for an old woman's advice about approaching this young beauty at your school. My advice is plain. If you love her, tell her. I cannot make it plainer. If you love her, tell her. Spill the beans, as your grandfather would say. It did not continue between him and I, but still I will love him for all of my days.

He called me his blancmange. I called him my potato, because he was versatile and his collars were very well starched. In French we say *tu me manques*: you are missing to me. The beloved is put first and not the self. Put the beloved first. Write to this girl of your feelings. Let the beans be spilled. But do not bother to enclose any of your drawings.

Your grandmother

## Keeping Mummy

In nineteen-seventy we come
to Bristol city, 'cos my mum
has seen an advert for some rows
of brand new chalet bungalows
at knockdown prices in The West,
and mum knows bungalows are best.
My dad has just retired from work,
but not a man to rest or shirk
he takes up all the household chores.
He does the carpet on all fours.
He empties bins, he fills the shelves
while mum, the younger of themselves,
she gets a Mini, eight-years-old,
she gets a man to paint it gold.
And once a week her hair is dressed,
inside the chalet in The West,
and once a month she takes the test
to lose the pesky Learner's plate.
It takes a while, it's worth the wait,
then Gladys comes to add to this,
from Canada to see her sis,
and this completes my mother's bliss.
So many years since they last clapped
their eyes and hands and overlapped.
And Glad flies home and when she's gone,
my mum she drives the motor on.
The key is curled, the world ignites.
She drives and dad, he dips the lights.

# The Adventures
of Monsieur Robinet

(2009)

# The Adventures of Monsieur Robinet

One morning, in the baker's, Madame Toutmoi says to Monsieur Robinet, 'Ah, hello, my sausage. I am going to Paris on the train next Saturday. You are most welcome to accompany me.'

'Thank you, but it is not possible,' answers Robinet. 'Next Saturday I am washing my dog.'

\*

Monsieur Robinet is in his shed with his dog. The man is repairing his bicycle. The dog puts his nose in the box of tools. 'Not in my tools, Chirac,' says Monsieur Robinet. 'Not unless you know how to repair a puncture.'

\*

One afternoon in the garden, with his father's old spade, Monsieur Robinet digs a big hole. Into the ground he puts Chirac's kennel. Unseen, his neighbour watches from the window upstairs.

The job completed, Robinet says to his dog 'You are not to dig it up... Good dog.'

\*

Monsieur Robinet is visiting his brother in England. His friend, Monsieur Raymond, gives food to Chirac during his master's absence. He also repairs Monsieur Robinet's television. It is Christmas. Monsieur Robinet has a gift for his niece. It is a little plastic dog. The dog speaks. It says 'Where is my kennel?'

\*

Monsieur Robinet comes home from his holiday and buries his luggage in the garden. His neighbour watches from the window. When Robinet has finished his work he sits beside his dog on a pile of stones. After a few moments he remembers that his pear is hidden in his baggage, in one of his shoes.

\*

'Monsieur Robinet… Hello… Now… do you want to come and see my new dog?' says Madame Toutmoi, on the telephone.

'A new dog!' exclaims Chirac's owner, interested. 'What is it called?'

'It is called Mitterrand,' she replies.

'A very good name,' says Monsieur Robinet. 'Yes…very good.'

\*

One day Monsieur Robinet is busy beating his television when there is a knock knocking at his door. It is Madame Toutmoi. 'Mitterrand has disappeared,' she cries.

'Please excuse me,' answers Robinet, going out into the garden to make sure that Chirac has not disappeared also. He then returns indoors, ready to join the search.

\*

In the evening, it snows. During the night, it freezes. In the morning, as usual, Monsieur Robinet goes to the shop to buy a pear for his breakfast. In front of his home the pavement is like a mirror and he slips to the ground. Arriving at the shop he says to the shopkeeper 'Two packets of salt, please. It's for the frozen pavement.'

'Don't you want a pear?' asks the shopkeeper.

'Oh, yes. For a moment I forgot,' replies Robinet.

The shopkeeper hits him with a potato. 'Tomorrow you will not forget.'

Perhaps you do not understand why the shopkeeper has a potato. It's for when the wind comes through the door. Without the potato the newspapers fly into the air like big birds.

Outside the shop Monsieur Robinet meets Madame Toutmoi. 'Hello,' she says to him. 'I am cold. Poor me. February isn't the month for me. Why have you got a lot of salt? For your pear?'

'No,' replies Monsieur Robinet. 'It is for the pavement.'

'What!' cries Madame Toutmoi. 'Me, I cannot believe it. You are going to eat the pavement! Monsieur Robinet, you will always be a mystery to me.'

\*

Today Monsieur Robinet makes his contribution to the town festival. Carefully he places pebbles on the grass, forming the letters of a message for the people: TELEVISION IS BAD FOR YOUR CONVERSATION WITH THE DOG. His dog quietly keeps guard over his master's pile of pebbles.

\*

Monsieur Robinet's niece is making a visit. At breakfast she says, 'Uncle, do you say the *end* of the bread or the *beginning*?'

'I say the beginning of the bread,' answers her uncle.

'And what about your dog, Chirac?' asks the niece. 'What does he say?'

'My dog does not speak,' replies Monsieur Robinet.

\*

Monsieur Robinet is invited for dinner at the home of Madame Toutmoi. He is very unhappy. The last time he paid her a visit he only said three words: 'Hello', 'thank you' and 'goodbye'. Oh, all right... four words. All the time Madame Toutmoi had said 'Me this...' and 'Me that...' Me, me, me. Afterwards he decided, never again. But when she telephoned him with another invitation he said 'Yes, yes, but of course. A dinner at your home... great!'

The day of his visit arrives. He gets up happy. Why? Because he has a sickness. His nose is dripping. He picks up the telephone. 'Madame...' After ten me-minutes he recommences. 'I'm gutted, Madame. I've got a cold. I need to stay at home today.'

'But Monsieur Robinet,' she replies. 'I've bought a big pear for you.'

'A big pear!' says Monsieur Robinet. 'Madame Toutmoi, I'm coming. I will bring my handkerchief.'

\*

One Sunday afternoon Monsieur Robinet and his dog are in the park. It begins to rain. 'Excuse me, Chirac,' says Robinet, putting his dog on his head to provide protection against the cloud wet. The priest who passes says 'Let us not ask questions about that which is above us.'

\*

Madame Toutmoi rings Monsieur Robinet. 'For my birthday I have asked Monsieur Raymond to take me out in his car for a picnic. Can you come? Bring your dog,' says Madame Toutmoi, '... and your money.'

\*

Monsieur Robinet is out dog-walking when he realises that all the colours are mixed up. The cows are green. Green! They walk under a blue sun and a yellow sky. Monsieur Robinet takes his pear out of his bag and the fruit is grey – grey with stripes of violet, orange and black. He eats the pear. Madame Toutmoi approaches and says, 'Monsieur Robinet, I need you. Desperately.' Monsieur Robinet is embarrassed. Suddenly Madame Toutmoi turns into an enormous potato. Monsieur Robinet places her in his bag and returns home to prepare his dinner.

\*

Monsieur Robinet is trying to make his dog speak. He holds a bone and says to the creature, 'Chirac, this is not a kennel – what is it?' The dog continues to sleep.

\*

Mr Robinet answers the telephone and hears the voice of Madame Toutmoi. 'What a lovely day. Would you like to go into the country for a cycle ride?'

'Today, no!' replies Robinet. 'Today I am washing my handkerchief.'

\*

One night Monsieur Robinet buries the kennel of his dog in the garden. When he has finished his work he eats a pear.

After the meal, under a scrap of the moon, the man digs up Chirac's little home, and for three hours the dog speaks its joy.

# Monsieur Robinet's short drama for the town festival

*Performed by Monsieur Robinet, Chirac and Monsieur Raymond.*
*The two men are wearing potato sacks*


Monsieur Raymond: It's not far now, my friends.

Monsieur Robinet: I hope not, Antoine, my torch is burning... and so is my rheumatism. Why are we climbing this hill? I hope there is something at the top.

Monsieur Raymond: You have hope. That is good. Here we are... Look! Our banquet.

Monsieur Robinet: But it is just a pile of pebbles!

Monsieur Raymond: We have forgotten the importance of stones, Antoine. Take the stone of Arthur, for example.

Monsieur Robinet: Arthur?

Monsieur Raymond: Arthur... who took out the sword Excalibur which was imprisoned in the stone. Only the future king could do it. But he took the sword and left what was important: the stone. The usual mistake. We cannot see the moon for the sunshine. He left the big prize. The stone! The most important thing. The more ordinary thing.

Monsieur Robinet: And the most heavy!

Monsieur Raymond: The stone was in fact an enormous potato.

Monsieur Robinet: Really...? And this pile, here... are they pebbles or small potatoes?

Monsieur Raymond: They are neither. They are dog biscuits.

Chirac: Really...?

FROM

# Uncut Confetti

(2006)

# A Make-over Mistake

There's a photo of my father, I think it's Monte Carlo, I'd say the 1930s. A young man fired up and dashing, in spatted shoes and cravat. In the Seventies and *his* sixties, when he was retired, I thought it would be a good idea if he could be a little more trendy. Just because he was getting old didn't mean he had to look like he'd lost it. So, he and I went to Bristol city centre and bought tank tops and purple flared trousers. Also, at my behest, he grew his sideburns. When the changes were complete, I didn't say anything because I didn't want to offend him, but I thought we had made an error. And perhaps because he didn't want to offend me either, only very gradually did he ease back into the man he had once been.

# Baby at Work

She is one.
She is having fun.
Everything's a skittle
or in the wrong place.
Surfaces are to be cleared.
Milk is to be spilt
not cried about.
Crying is for getting stuff:
attention, biscuits, the pencil full of poem.
The soil in the houseplants
is there to be spread
around the carpet.
Glasses don't belong on tables, or the face,
and parents do not belong in the bed.

# Messiah

This messiah walks into a bar
and asks for a drink of tap water.
'Why don't you *buy* a drink for a change,
instead of changing water into one?'
says the barman.
'Buy one? What with?' asks the messiah.
'How come you never have any money?'
'Because I don't believe in it.'
'What *do* you believe in?'
'I believe in *you*. I love *you*.'
'Don't give me that,
you buy a drink or you get out.'
'Oh, come on, what does a drink of water cost?'
'It cost me labour to pour it.
You take up space to drink it,
then I have to wash the cup up after you.
And what if you break it?
Who pays then?'
'I could mend it.'
'Perform a miracle, you mean?
And have everyone crowding around in amazement
and *not buying drinks*? No, thanks.
Out.'

## Glasgow Window

Awaiting the shuttle bus
from Glasgow Central
to take us
to Queen Street Station,
across the road's divide,
a man inside a shop window.
I thought, he must know me,
or why else would he be waving?
Further scrutiny invests the gent's gesture
with other meaning:
he is not waving,
but window cleaning.

# Getting in a Lava

The Frenchman, Patrice, is preceded
by a reputation for mapping and snapping volcanoes.
I am told it is not his work, but his passion.
Getting to meet the man
around a French mealtime table
at the home of his sister, Cecile,
he intimates that canyons
also get him and his camera going.
I indicate the steep sides
which canyons and volcanoes have in common.
His sister indicates a brother always reeling
on the edge of a precipice of some sort.
A man on the edge.

Fruit is offered for desert.
Patrice proceeds
to pare the apple peel with his pocket knife,
and as he uses it again,
to divide the flesh,
it triggers a forgotten flash of my father.
Him sat at our mealtime table with his own pen knife,
generously giving me the best slice
from hands cracked to angry canyons
and salved with Vaseline.
Dad, you were sometimes ready to erupt,
but in spite of any scalding spanking which you gave me,
I was never in any doubt
that you would unquestioningly sacrifice
the rest of your life
to save me.

## His Little Bit on the Side

Now and then she liked to give
her hubby something funny with his grub.
In his packed lunch
she put a punch line,
chucking him a chuckle
in his lunchtime,
something that would tickle
with the cheese and pickle sandwiches.
From time to time
she packed a punch line
with an orange
or Satsuma from the sun
in his packed lunch –
a pithy punch line.
Why should Christmas crackers have all the fun?
She wanted to know, she wanted to know
the difference between God and a potato
... *God may be an all-seeing*
*infinite, omnipresent being,*
*but He's not as good as potatoes are*
*with chives and mayonnaise,*
*and spuds don't get much of a look in on* Songs of Praise.
*But they should do.*
*They ought to.*

# Mr Cooper Continued

*This piece began as a response to the poem 'Mr Cooper' by Anthony Thwaite, in which the poem's narrator recounts a visit to a Manchester pub in the 1960s. He finds a jeweller's card left on a shelf above a lavatory urinal. Turning it over, he discovers the words 'MR COOPER DEAD' written in thick pencil. He leaves the pub disconcerted by this stark reminder of mortality.*

*With a less formal structure, my own piece takes up the voice in the poem, in 1960s Manchester.*

So, he was dead,
the card had said.
Back in the hotel
that calling card
was on my mind, indelibly.
Such hard words
for so soft a pencil.
So few words
to cancel
Mr Cooper.
Who was he?
An ardent call within me said:
find out what you can
about the man,
pick up the thread.
An so next day,
washed, brushed and breakfasted,
other work, which I had planned, would wait.
I'd be a Mr Cooper snooper,
of sorts.
So where would my investigating eye first fall?
The jeweller should be worth a call, obviously,
but it's a trait
of mine
to mine
where it's less obvious:
oblivious
to the obvious.
That's me,
occasionally.

That Manchester morning,
the spring was in the air
and in my step,
the schlep of discovery ahead.
In a public library reading room
I grazed the local press,
unearthing the only Mr Cooper
reported meeting maker
in the region round that time.
A reference volume rendered an address.
I dipped out into the afternoon,
found a bus to Hulme.
Our conductor knew the street
and advised me of a short cut.
I dipped off in the advised direction but
quickly went askew.
I could have bought a map, of course,
but more can sometimes happen
with the littler we do.
Although, on this occasion,
I just spent a long time wandering aimlessly.

Back on track,
the designated door I knocked,
Mrs Cooper wasn't shocked.
She understood my need to trace him,
felt it must be fate,
asked me in,
his full-length photo lent above the grate.
I complemented her former husband's looks,
admired his hat.
'His hats were always top,' she opted.
I wondered what was that
sat at his photoed feet?
Was it a huge potato?
'No, it's a dog.'
Our dialogue continued.
'It's out in the kitchen as we speak,
he kept it like a king.'

'A King Edward?' I suggested.
She suggested I curtail potato talk
and take the creature for a walk.

The kitchen door open,
the dog streaked through.
'I can barely bear to look at him,
it brings to mind his master!' she sighed.
'...Would you care to have the dog yourself?
He's got a licence, he's injected
and he's wormed.'
I explained my home was short on space,
'I'll take him for a walk, though,'
I confirmed.
I decided to walk the animal substantially.
An eight or nine hour job, I reckoned:
give Mrs Cooper an obvious break.

As I approached her porch a second time,
a church bell chimed the ten,
I'd had to take the beast
shouldered for at least the last two hours.
The door opened, the dog barked.
The creature and me
came through to the settee.
'Thanks for doing him.
He likes a nice long one,
but who doesn't,' she observed jokingly.
'I've made you a packed lunch, by the way.'
It seemed late for packed lunching
but any foodstuff was welcome enough,
I'd not touched a crumb since brekky.
A reccy of my parcel
revealed an orange
and some silver foil enclosing no more than a sliver of egg.
Mrs Cooper explained
that it had previously contained bread
and full filling,
but she'd eaten it.

'You've still got the *idea* of a sandwich though,' I was advised,
which I found not depressing
but thrilling.
I'd been unwilling to address my drawn-ness
to this woman.
But now I'd stop,
for she too was top.
She had an expansive point of view
which you could just smell.
She had the stench of anarchist enchantment about her.
Yes, she reeked havoc.

She offered further food,
'Have a fig roll...'
'Lovely, yes, thank you.'
I wasn't mad keen on the fig roll scene
but I didn't want to be rude, and who does?
And why?
'Think of it as your little bit on the side,' she said.
She told me how her husband
had once been a hat-blocker in Stockport.
'... The trade's dying though,' she added,
with evident pain at mortality's mention.
'I'm sorry about your husband, Mr Cooper.
May I ask you, how did he die?'
She told me that he'd choked on a fig roll.
I told her I was sorry.
She said, 'It wasn't horrible,
he died laughing, you know.'
'... Laughing and choking,' I offered.
'... That's right,' she accepted.

I must admit,
my fire was well and warmly lit by the woman.
But as I tucked into my imaginary sandwiches
I became resistant.

*No, no – don't go down that way,*
*you know where there's a spark*
*the dark is not far distant,*
*you know that heaven is twinned with hell.*
*You know that it can only*
*go lonely...*
'Don't be stupid,'
reproved the cupid within,
and I made my move.
'Can I kiss you, Mrs Cooper?'
'Call me Alice,' she answered plainly.
Our swelling kiss completed, she said,
'Don't do that again.'

I had hoped she might have said:
*Move up to Manchester,*
*I've been waiting for you.*
*Move up to Manchester,*
*that's what you've got to do.*
*More love to Manchester,*
*that's what you've got to bring – your love to Manchester,*
*make more of Manchester sing.*
*Move up to Manchester,*
*come and share my abode.*
*Move up to Manchester,*
*up the Liverpool Road.*
*Move up to Manchester,*
*come and be where I am,*
*Move up to Manchester,*
*or at least to Altrincham.*
But she didn't.

'He was so many things to me,' she confided.
'He was the lover of my life,
He was my fresh tomato ketchup,
He was the mustard on my pie,
He was the eye of my potato. Yes, potato,' she smiled.

'He was the life and party of my soul,
He was the sole priest of my amazement,
He was the line of my horizon,
He was my stuff bought from the buffet,
He was my cup of borrowed sugar,
He was my favourite Liquorice Allsort,
He was my grass from Honolulu,
He was my dog dirt of good fortune,
He was my unexpected downpour,
He was the apple of the orders of my doctor.'

I asked her, 'Was he your funny little face cloth?
Was he your corrugated ironing board?'
Mrs Cooper replied
that he was many things,
but not these two.

## Stick Man

Before you set to
with that thin bamboo,
you always asked us if we knew
*why* you were caning us.
One boy was told to go to you for treatment
because his own teacher couldn't hit him hard enough.
He got your usual question,
'You know why I'm doing this?'
Absentmindedly the boy answered, 'Yes, Miss.'

Whenever you overshot your informed target,
the stick would make a flappy sound
against your trouser leg,
although such errors did not count
towards the canee's allotted amount.
You always gave us the full whack.

But then you touched us in a softer way,
day after day, a clutch of your favourite poems,
always the same ones, in the same order.
And I thank you for banging in
that bing bang bongo lingo,
I'm grateful to you for hammering home
those gems in the wordpile,
that jawed magic.
And I'll remember you, if I can,
without your stick.
You were a man
with severe teaching difficulties.

## Minotaur

In the myth,
in the deep down maze of the cave,
he went to find the minotaur.
And before he went,
he took a reel of twine:
a trick to traipse the return trip
back to the world of sense and sunshine.
It was sound thinking:
be enticed by new chance and challenge
but keep in touch
with your place of origin.
Don't let your past be lost,
or it'll cost
your future.

# Orpheus and the Animals

I was slack,
I looked back.
Now I've nothing to look forward to.

Now you creatures
are my teachers.
You give me a lesson in how
to live all my life in the now.

Mind you,
when I feel like a bit of a chat,
you're useless.

## 2B 2½

In the brasserie for breakfast,
the artist puts his pencil
in her small and restless hand.
Pulling over a serviette,
he says to get drawing.
The child gets drawing,
but over and beyond the designated area.
The table is now marked with lead.
No, not on the table, says the artist,
only draw on the paper.
And the bread.

## Wild Bunch

When I was a child,
my dad called me various names.
A Bunch of M'galoop was my favourite.
Not a bunch of M'galoops,
no, just the one...
You can't have a bunch of one,
can you?
Unless you're just having fun.
And we were.
It sounded like a feast
for an unusual African beast.
An animal whose life was free.
An astonishing creature
whose eyes were pools
in which fools could see
the infinite
without it being scary.

## Zen Dad

When I asked my father why he'd stopped painting,
he told me, 'You children are my paintings now.'
The brushes down, he became a gardening man.
Moving homes, there were the various wildernesses for him to tame.
Thick brick-a-bramble challenges,
which he brought into line.
Brushing with nature,
brushing the paths,
blushing with effort.
Pinks and nasturtiums,
string and bamboo,
border plants and beans,
the fork and the trowel,
trod and turned
long beyond daylight.
'I don't know what he does out there,'
said mum.
If you'd really pressed her
she'd have guessed, I think:
time alone,
the creation of order,
communion with God.
On the last occasion,
he came indoors complaining of pains in the chest.
Mum suggested he'd best lie down.
'I'll just go and put my tools away,' he answered,
which he did.
Back in again,
lying on the sofa
he slipped away from the world and the woman
he loved as one.
The job
well and truly,
and very tidily,
done.

# The Sound of Paint Drying

(2003)

# Left-footed Poem

My left foot at football
was my least good.
Being as my right foot was bad,
this meant that my left foot
was very bad.
There were occasions, though,
when a combination
of self-belief and bravado
had me use my very bad foot
with thunderous accuracy.
On one occasion in Kilkenny,
during a match between comedians,
Ireland against The Rest of the World,
we, the non-Irish,
were an embarrassing 7-2 down
when the ball came whizzing my way
and I had an impulse to play
the left-footed dilettante,
and the ball flew emphatically, unstoppably
beyond the reach of the flailing goalkeeper.
My own goalkeeper.
And I took ownership of that goal
instead of feeling small:
I celebrated what I had done.
We were, after all,
comedians.

# By Rail, Scotland

I am sitting on the train opposite an attractive woman of maybe eighty. We have been chatting cheerfully. She is Mrs Phelps, Mrs Dora Phelps. She is on her way back from a Christian singles weekend. One phrase in her description of the event sticks with me: 'Fun and Fellowship.' She remains glued to the passing landscape, unwraps a sweet and is soon sucking fervently. I feel the conversation has been going well enough for me to ask her: 'Can I have one?' She looks at me directly for the first time now – 'No, get your own sweets.'

'Fun and fellowship... Like the Cathars,' I suggest.

'The Cathars?' says Mrs Phelps, pushing me back into the head-rest because I am obscuring the view of the landscape.

I nod and continue. 'The Cathars were Christian heretics in the Middle Ages. A million wiped out by Simon de Montfort, a million!'

'How strange,' she says, '...so exact a number.'

She speaks of the Second Coming and says she wishes the Lord would 'rattle his dags' and get down here. I ask her what dags are and she says that it is best not to ask.

She gives me details of the next gathering, writing the address on a sweet wrapper. I wonder what sort of pen she is using that writes so readily on wax paper. She hands me a photograph of herself wearing merely a pair of pants. 'That's me, half a century ago, when I was twenty-six.'

I feel an impossible desire, which is at the same time infinitely comforting. I think of the song recently released by The Beautiful South, which boasts the unwitherable beauty of the eyes.

As we pull into her station we exchange phone numbers, although I give her the wrong one because it's all a bit too frightening.

# Eurydice Speaks

Dog calmed,
river crossed –
the gods had made it so clear:
look back and she's lost.
So, dog calmed, river crossed,
why did he look back?
Was it a chance over-shoulder glance,
an absent-minded oversight
that sent me back to Hades,
or was it him checking
to see that I was still there
and then knowing
in that moment of knowing
that I was
but wouldn't be,
or was it an upbraiding glare,
petulance at my following him,
an impulsive reprimand
for which he would reprimand himself
for the rest of his days?
Or was it that he just went nuts?

Or was it a celebratory sharing,
his foot upon the threshold,
he turns...
'Eurydice, look – we're there...'
And then only *he* is there.
The overenthusiastic folly.
The premature judgement.
The complacent Greek.
What was his mistake?
The mistake is yours
if you look only at the possible errors of the man.
With the woman lies the solution.
Yes, it happened at the very threshold.
But he turned because...

because I called him.
And why?
Because I wanted to look at him once more,
but once only.

# Australia, Christmas, 2001

Me, Simon and the farm lorry go
down the mountain road from Dorrigo,
rattling through rainforest
in the ute,
en route to Lennox Head
and its Christmas spread of surf.
Simon is at the steering wheel,
our eyes similarly imperfect.
At the beach, under the sun,
I slip my glasses into my swimwear pocket
and dip into the frothing lip of ocean,
but the tide slips inside
and whips away my glasses.
Keen-eyed Janet is good enough
to dive into the sea's heaving haystack,
but they're good and gone.
So, maybe I've made some myopic mermaid better looking.

With no spare pair available
and no optician seeing customers on Christmas day,
Simon is open to a timeshare with his own pair.
Hooray.
My co-wearer's prescription is of different description,
but if I tip them at an angle
and don't pull them full on,
the wool over my eyes unstitches;
we're a bit like Shakespeare's witches,
who had just one eye between them,
but there's only two of us
and we're not in Scotland,
we're in Australia,
sharing optical regalia.

# October '71

Today, on my eighteenth birthday,
my dad gave me a hefty gift in coloured wrapping.
The deftly-sealed paper gone,
the black tin box revealed
my father's oil paints.
Inside – the well-thumbed wood of his palette.
I have asked him why he gave up
and here is my answer. He gave up for me to go on.
Here is creativity's baton.
Eyeing the palette, I contemplate
the crusty daubs and splodges
of his concocted shades.
I investigate the metal tubes of pigment.
They are rock solid
and have been so for decades.

# The Sound of Paint Drying

*On my wall there is a small picture of a street scene in France, painted long before I was born, by an amateur watercolourist. The focus is a five-storey vine-clad building with a bar at the bottom; the name is visible on the sign – Le Bar de la Treille – the bar with the trellis. There are a couple of barrels and a quintet of people. Facing the bar is a brown-hatted man. There is blue sky, there are green railings. In the bottom right-hand corner is the artist's signature: R. Hegley,* Vieux Nice (1931).

The picture I usually paint of my father
is the one of him smacking me as a lad:
hard and uncompromising.
It is not a lie but neither is it the only angle
from which one can capture his portrait.

Other brush strokes reveal a man born in France,
to a French mother – a man who, in his twenties,
made gentle, playful, colourful paintings of his native land.

In 1905
my dad was alive
but he wasn't alive before this.
His mum used to dance with the Folies-Bergère
and she was a native of Paris.

My grandad gave my father
his Anglo-Irish name,
it seems he gave him little else,
which is a shame,
but I don't apportion blame;
grandma called her son René Robert,
although Bob's what he later became.

My father painted canvases,
his mum played mandolin:
the artiness was in the blood
and sometimes on the skin.

*

We find my father sat in Nice
when he was twenty-six,
he's poking at some canvas
with his range of hairy sticks.
First he takes his pencil
and he outlines what he sees;
proportion and perspective by degrees,
then turning to his brushes,
to the narrow and the stout,
he puts them in the pigment
as he wiggles them about.
And it's highly naturalistic,
it is not impressionistic,
it is not expressionistic,
neither futurist nor fauve.
It isn't pointillistic,
it is highly naturalistic.
In places it is orange
and in others it is mauve.


4 May 2001


On the plane to Nice from Luton. My intention is to paint the scene
my father painted, or whatever scene is in its place. If the whole
street has been turned into an office, then I will paint the wall. I
have a sore throat. I have a supply of Strepsils. Normally I buy
the red ones – Strepsils Originals – but for my French visit I have
gone for yellow Strepsils. I believe life favours the one who takes
risks. I have no painting equipment: I will purchase it in France.

Why do I embark upon this journey?

To take up my father's tools.

To know the fixing of line and the mixing of colour as he knew it.

To visit the town I know he loved.

I cherish the fragment of Frenchness which I have through my
father's birthplace (Paris), his name (René) and his French mother
(Maman). In doing this painting I hope to claim something of this
inheritance, and to find out by treading in my father's footsteps
something about my own feet.

5 May

Nice.

My paints I purchase from a shop patronised by Matisse himself – and possibly by my own old master. I joke with the vendor about the expense of his equipment, his pencils in particular, adding that at least the water will be free. He is only very mildly amused.

Seeking out the site of my father's creation I find the same street and the same bar are still in place – the bar has a new name, but there is the very vine which clawed its way up his watercolour, seventy years previous. And there is the same iron railing whose intricacies he wrought. And still it is painted green. The whole of this ancient part of town is much as he left it; the most noticeable modern addition is the graffiti – cosmetic, although you wouldn't want it on your face.

6 May

I set up with my equipment outside what was once Le Bar de la Treille. It is a sunny morning. My throat is more sore; still, I have had my coffee and curved croissant. It is ten o'clock. I set my pad upon my knee, I open my clean array of oblong colours. When asked for a pencil in the shop, the patron recommended 5H – *very hard*; I didn't want to contradict generations of experience and followed his direction. But I also bought a 5B pencil – a Mister Softy. I want my formative lines to be clear. I look at the leafy building before me, I survey its angles. I consider its shadows. I get the sense of it, as my old dad would have done. I begin.

\*

My father's painting is very traditional and also very competent. What is of particular note is the working of the detail, as though it's been done on a massive scale and then reduced accordingly – as though the tiny is home. As I make my piece I realise my shortcomings as a brush master. I get despondent early on, but stay with it. And then, working on the sky, as I pop a new yellow Strepsil into my mouth to ease my aching, I know what I must do. Out comes the Strepsil and onto my newly painted blueness it goes. Mixed-media – watercolour and throat sweet. And the sun is in the sky, and the son understands his place in things. Not the fine brush worker, the steady builder – that was my dad. I go on with renewed incentive. Don't just know your limitations. Love them.

My father was a painter. I am an idiot.

\*

1.00 p.m. Outdoors at a nearby restaurant, awaiting some lunch, the sun smiles upon my near-completed painting which I'm looking at now upon my lap. In the interval before my meal's arrival I decide to put a figure on the street. I decide to depict the hatted man from my father's painting. The same man but, unlike dad, I depict him with his back to the café, facing front. After much fiddling, the man is finished. I realise that he is me. He doesn't look much like me, but nor does my painting of the street look much like the street. The man is me. I draw him a dog.

And that's why I came here. For an art of necessity. I painted this picture to find myself. I found myself. *And* my dog.

After lunch, I return to the scene, to add the last details to my piece. Someone from a café opposite the one I'm painting comes and has a look. He seems affirmative. He indicates that he has other paintings of the voluptuous vine inside. I discover that they are mostly more modern, but there is one that is older. 1930. It is a colour copy. The signature in the bottom right-hand corner is R. Dufy – French fauvist, Raoul Dufy.

Something which has come to light as my own work has progressed is the physical point of view of my father's painting. It would seem to be not from the street, but from the window of the building opposite. I have little detail of his life at this time. I knew he was here with my grandmother. Is this where they lived? A sequence of events suggests itself: one morning, a year before he paints the scene, my father looks out of the window and sees below him a man at work with watercolours. This other man seems happy, engrossed, fulfilled. Like I have been. But it is not me. It is not necessary for my father to find me through some ludicrous somersault of time. It is Dufy whom my father watches.

Perhaps my father has never yet put his thumb through the palette; but now he is hooked. I'll have some of that, he thinks, in French, and the following year he is at it himself, after an argument with the man in the art shop about the extortionate price of his pencils.

\*

Last night I picked my father's painting off the wall. I had still believed there to be only four figures outside that bar. I now knew there to be five. Now the woman was stooping over her wares with a sale a possibility. Previously she had merely been stooping, maybe looking at some flowers, maybe rearranging them, but now she would seem to be entering into a process of exchange. This insubstantial man would seem to be spending money. We make our guesses and our assumptions. He is glad of good value. He is probably buying flowers, possibly fruit, maybe pencils. Cheap pencils.

\*

I have been asked what is inside the two barrels
resting on the pavement.

Let me tell you.
In the barrels
there are bees.
Stripy bees.

The woman in the stripy apron
is shortly to turn
and free
the barrelled bee-life.
She'll make a bee-line
for the bee-life
in what used to be the tree-life,
with her knife.
And the man
at the front of it all
is still trying to comprehend
her beauty,
a man who has never travelled up the Eiffel Tower.

'It is every Frenchman's duty,' he will say,
asking her to accompany him
up to that famous above
where he'll fall in love with her
and call her sweet, so sweet – his blancmange.

Suddenly a hurled potato breaches
a window in Le Bar de la Treille.
The owner rapidly appears in search of a culprit.
The leaning man indicates the ripped face
peering from the pasted poster.
'It was him!' he accuses, in the lingo of France,
whilst beginning to dance.
'It's nothing to dance about! Nothing!'
opposes the patron.

'Dancing needs not wait upon occasion,
it is the natural state of the human animal,'
explains the dancing man.
The bar proprietor returns to his domain,
picks up the offending potato,
holds it to his ear
and listens
to the sound of the ground
from whence it came.

# The New Father's Mistake

In the hospital,
the new mother has agreed
to assist in testing the worth
of a new natal drug.
Soon after the birth,
the marvellous midwife gives me the relevant questionnaire to hold
and proceeds to organise her patient's relative comfort.
I mistakenly think she has told me to complete
the sheet.
Inwardly I express surprise
that my responses are of interest, but feel it best
not to question the interests of modern science.
I proceed to give my answers in
dutiful compliance.
Marking is from nought to five
depending on how intensely
the phenomenon described
is thought to have been experienced.
The following represents how it was for me.
Headaches – nought
Abdominal pain – nought
Nausea – nought
Shivering – nought
Vomiting – nought
Tiredness – five

# The Party Spirito

A lovely hilltop village party
above the seaside of Sestri Levante:
Beer, Chianti,
aubergine, spaghetti
and pesto on bread like chapatti.
The band play the cha-cha
and what sounds to me like Italian village party music.
They play it well.
The partygoers swell
to maybe six hundred.
The time is after ten.
Now we leave, to spread the small children
in their bedtime.
Hermione, who is two,
has a question:
'What about the candles?'
It is understandable.
It is a party, after all.
Approaching the cars
she says she wants to blow them out.
She is referring to the stars.

# The Knowledge

I have known a love
which was true.
I have been beautiful
in the eyes of the beautiful.
I have been kissed by the lips I longed for.
I have seen heaven
in the eyes of the beholder.
I have been home.

# Dog

(2000)

# Classic

In the radio interview,
the former Classics student
asked me about the similarity between
my writings and those of Aristotle.
I said I didn't know there was such a similarity.
When she asked how useful my Sociology degree had been,
I answered that it had taught me how to felt-tip
my idea of a potato on to a sheet of transparent plastic
then compare it with the real world
by placing it over an existing potato.
She said, 'That's Plato.'

# The Death of the Potatoes

In the monastery kitchen
my job has been to sort out the potatoes.
On the shelves overhead,
the broad serving plates
and the hoard of diminishing saucepans.
The brown jackets
I have removed religiously.
Fist tight-shut around the cord-bound tool,
I have revealed their inner selves,
cutting and gouging wherever required.
Once peeled and poked eyeless
I have quartered them
and commended them to the heat
and the slaughter
upon the stove.
I kneel beneath the steaming,
my eyes are streaming.
Brother Matthew enters.
He questions my pose.
I tell him I pray for the souls of the potatoes.

# The Law According to Neck

Our French master was given the nickname
of Neck
because he was blessed
with a heck of a distance
between the bottom of his face
and the top of his chest.
When we were marking our neighbour's vocabulary test,
Neck would always lay down
very specific guidelines for the task.
These he referred to as his four simple rules:
If it's not right, it's wrong.
If it's not there, it's wrong.
If you can't read it, it's wrong.
And if it's not wrong, it's right.

## Unacceptable Social Exchange

Recently, in a public lavatory, I had just finished having a wee when a young man holding a sleeping toddler came and stood in the urinal stall beside me. With only one hand free he could not get the necessary purchase on his zip and I asked if he would like me to do it for him. The man became defensive. I had apparently crossed the line between assistance and interference. There are times, however, when unsolicited help is unlikely to be refused. The person running for a bus will not complain if you keep it waiting for them, although they will if you ask them for financial reward. And rightly so, no contract has been entered into. The person who asks someone for directions and gets no joy will not usually mind if you say you overheard them asking and can help. If you say you overheard them asking and cannot help either, they will be less grateful.

Certain information, although appropriate, can still be unwelcome. I once heard a chap in a bar asking a friend about a tonic for haemorrhoids. I excused my eavesdropping and listed four or five excellent creams and ointments as well as an old remedy using herbs placed in a saucepan of boiling water, which you then sat upon. Before I got on to explaining that care should be taken not to overfill the vessel, I was silenced by the irritated sufferer, who funnily enough was the same bloke I'd met in the public lavatory.

## Key Poem

Being a key
is my curse.
I live on a ring,
in a purse
or a pocket,
rarely seeing
my true home.
Only for a moment,
when I unlock it.

## Say It Now

Don't hold on till it's time to go
before you let your emotional side show,
don't hold on until tomorrow,
don't hold on for another moment.
Saying I love you's not original,
but nor is never letting someone know.
Why leave it till it's almost time to say the last goodbye
before you get to say the big hello?
Don't hang on till the gate is closing,
don't hang on till the daisies grow.
Why wait until it's nearly far too late.
Why wait for another moment?
Do you feel at home with a heart that's hardly ever open?
Why keep it bottled up
when there's a genie hoping to get out,
to shout it out,
the thing you really should have spoken about by now.
Why keep it bottled up until that heart is broken?
Say it now, it's not a moment too soon,
say it now, don't wait until next July or June.
Say it now, don't wait for the next eclipse of the moment.
One wish: no feeling will dilly-dally.
One wish: no lagging with love to show.
One wish: don't be an emotional scallywag,
you silly so-and-so.

# The Snowman's Dog

Up in Grange-over-Sands
we had love on our hands,
and with gloves on hands we went out in the snow
and we moulded and melded a dog from the snow.
And then on our back paws
we both went back indoors
and went up to the man at the desk.
And I asked him, 'Hey, did you know
there's a dog sitting out in the snow?'
And the man at the desk, he said, 'Oh!'
And he went and he opened a window
and he spoke to the dog in the snow.
He said, 'Snow dog, you haven't a kennel,
snow dog, you haven't a flannel
for wiping the tears that will flow.'
We left him and went up the stairs
and we sat on our chairs
and looked down on the dog from our window.
And with night drawing in
we began drawing him,
the dog, not the man down below,
which appeared on the snow of our pages,
out of the lead of our pencils.
And yours was 2B
and mine was 2B,
and I said we were 2B together,
and you told me 2B quiet.

# The Art of Advertising

Ladies and businessmen,
it is unlikely
that any reference
to your bank or beer,
or whatever,
will appear
in the finished commercial.
Not even by clever implication.
Your product is merely a starting point
providing finance
for fine art.
Let this be your reward.
Art cannot afford
to set its purpose
to the increase of corporate profile or profit.
Indeed the artist may see fit
to advertise a rival product
on your account,
to suit some compositional need.
Yes – we guarantee to induce no increase in your sales,
because the way the work is done
there will be no way of telling
which product it is you're selling:
no logo, no catchphrase,
no process of suggestion,
*no* glorification of consumerism
or the market economy whatsoever.
Art has higher things in mind.
To be doing well,
it must be ill-defined,
the BIG in ambiguity.
Let the artist choose.
You have nothing to lose
but your money.

## An Introduction to Folk

There're those who'd have you keep
folk songs for the sheep.
I shared such an aspersion
until immersion in a version
of a ballad by the name
of 'Anachie Gordon'
done by one Nic Jones.
John Peel it was,
who brought me to ken
the lingering longing
in the wavering tones
over intricate patterns
of the fingering bones, since when
many folk songs have moistened my eye,
and I can see why
the Morris dancer sports a spare hanky.

FROM

# Beyond Our Kennel

(1998)

# An Aeroplane Journey

He threw it at her in school assembly. He had assembled it during the sports notices. A page from the hymn book. It was her look he was after. Her look.

In his lap he flipped the tightly printed page into the tightly folded plane. She was in his head ninety-five per cent of his waking day and sixty-five per cent of his dreaming night. Sometimes he'd wanted to scream his fat infatuation when she was near. And sometimes he'd wanted to whisper it in her ear so gentle. Instead he'd put his energies into keeping a stifled mask of no interest whatsoever. Fear of rejection? Or just fear? Whatever it was, it was fearful. Now he was going to throw down the mask. He was going to let the throwing of the plane do the asking. 'How about a date? You're great!' he's written in the top margin and signed it.

Heads down for silent prayer; he knew that would be his moment. He took careful aim.

Fly! Fly, little arrow, to my heart's desire. To the source of this fire, fly, fly, little arrow, down a narrow corridor straight to your target. And the air was ridden and the message ended up where bidden. Silent, swift, unnoticed by the sundry and the all, falling, nestling in her spectacles. She took hold of the piece of paper and immediately caught sight of the handwriting so boldly put upon the wing. The name was a shock for sure. His dissembling had covered up his wonderment so well. She hadn't been able to see a single bubble of the cauldron burning up inside him. But she knew now. She knew just how the chemistry master felt about her. And she was a very happy head teacher indeed.

# The Beatles in Our Luton Bungalow

With the Beatles about
you had to admit
that it got better.
They put a hum
into the humdrum
and the drab.
Those four made us glad to be alive.
They made the five of us feel fab.
They were one of the three things
our family could appreciate together.
The other two were sleep
and oxygen.

# College Days

I study philosophy,
mixing with fellows
who mix their own muesli
and listen to cellos.

## Alien in Rouen

I've escaped to a school in Normandy
to lustre up my lingo.
The other students are mainly from Japan;
small, quiet and companionable.
One morning a new pupil appears.
He's a rugged giant of a man.
In the break for our coffee,
broken words through missing teeth
tell me that he is a Bosnian refugee.
He is unemployed and joined the class
to turn his situation about.
He could knock you into *semaine prochaine*
if he gave you a clout,
but he reads and writes French like an infant.
At the blackboard, the professor
teaches him how to spell the French word for 'without'.

# Nineteen Blessings

Blessèd be dogs.
Blessèd be dominoes.
Blessèd be black-eyes beans.
Blessèd be greens.
Blessèd be grit.
Blessèd be trampled confetti.
Blessèd be spoons.
Blessèd be spaghetti.
Blessèd be garden trowels.
Blessèd be hot towels in curry houses
that are really hot flannels.
Blessèd be kennels.
Blessèd be lead pencils, with or without rubbers.
Blessèd be scrubbers
which are sponge and scrubber combined.
Blessèd be letter boxes,
litter bins,
can-openers,
tin-openers
and the openness between us.
(All one blessing.)
Blessèd be sneezing.
Blessèd be snowmen.
Blessèd be concern for other people's snowmen.
Blessèd be our limitations.
Blessèd be carrots.

# Getting Away for Easter

Did he prefer his humour blue?
How old was he before he knew
the earthly job he had to do?
How many sugars in his brew?
He never got to make a pew,
nor had a sniff at sniffing glue,
but possibly he liked a brew,
and on occasions even threw
up over Judas and the crew,
he surely must have done a few
of the common things that people do,
and had he known the people who
would claim his name would he have grew
increasingly less likely to
get really stuck-up good and true.

If Jesus was of human kind,
with higher nature which defined
the end his father had in mind,
I ask if he'd have hung about
to let the blood come flooding out,
or would his task be to be gone
and leave the cross with nothing on,
would he have run from being racked
and done the disappearing act
before his hands and feet were tacked?
The word made flesh would he decide
'To let myself be crucified
foreknowing would be suicide,
and Lord knows that's a sin.
I'm not sure I can save the world
but God, I'll save my skin.'

# A Declaration of Need

I need you like a novel needs a plot.
I need you like the greedy need a lot.
I need you like a hovel needs a certain level of grottiness
to qualify.
I need you like acne cream needs spottiness.
Like a calendar needs a week.
Like a colander needs a leek.
Like people need to seek out what life on Mars is.
Like hospitals need vases.
I need you.
I need you like a zoo needs a giraffe.
I need you like a psycho needs a path.
I need you like King Arthur need a table
that was more than just a table for one.
I need you like a kiwi needs a fruit.
I need you like a wee wee needs a route out of the body.
I need you like Noddy needed little ears,
just for the contrast.
I need you like bone needs marrow.
I need you like straight needs narrow.
I need you like the broadest bean needs something else on the plate
before it can participate
in what you might describe as a decent meal.
I need you like a cappuccino needs froth.
I need you like a candle needs a moth
if it's going to burn its wings off.

# Some Resolutions

Some resolve to give up on the smoking
some resolve to cut out all the meat
some resolve to get their trunks more regularly soaking
and some resolve to stop all the deceit.
Some resolve to solve financial problems
by taking up a life involving crime
and some resolve to give their ageing parents
more than just the fag end of their time.
Some resolve to have a hobby
some resolve to join a lobby
some resolve to clear up every jobbie
that their doggie does
and not go hosepipe crazy in the drought
and some of the aforesaid resolutions
dissolve before the Christmas tree's been put outside the door,
especially resolutions one and four.

# Love Cuts

(1995)

# Skip

My dad escorted me to the hut,
the day I went along to join the cub scouts.
And after I had joined in some of the games,
Skip took us to one side, asked us both our names,
then asked me if I was enjoying myself.
And when I said that I was,
he told me that being a cub scout
was about having fun, but
it was also about duty, decency and paying your subscriptions.

And I looked at my dad because
he was listening like a little boy.
Looking back I think
Skip was like the father my father never had;
the protector, the advisor
and the authority above.
My dad was like a little lad with the gift of love.
He was in the grip
of Skip,
and when he got home he stated
that we had been in the presence of a great man.
And I felt sad
that the parent is only expected to attend on the recruit's first visit,
and I said 'I bet you wish you could go again yourself, Dad?'
And my dad said that I had a cheek
and that he would be going along every week.

# My Father Shows His Teeth

One morning my dad asked me to comb my hair
before leaving home for school.
And I said no,
then quickly picked up my blazer
and exited the bungalow.
Half way up the road
I heard running feet behind me.
I turned to find my father
chasing me with the comb
and a very red face.
I sped off, sure that his older frame
would lose in a race,
but his pace was made faster
by his need to show me who the master was.
And at the top of the street
he stopped me, stretching and grasping my collar
and spinning me hard against the wall.
For a while we stood together gasping.
Quietly he offered me the comb, telling me
that if I didn't tidy my hair
he'd come down the school
and do it for me in front of all my friends.
I didn't actually have any friends
but I thought it best to smarten myself up anyway.

# The Dog Smoggler

I sit in the gallery beside a man who is stroking an imaginary dog. An attendant comes over and asks him to remove the creature from the premises.

'But it's only a pretend dog,' I protest on the muttering man's behalf.

'I'm sorry,' replies the official, 'but the only pretend animals of any description which the gallery permits are confined to the exhibits.'

Then the man announces that his dog has had an accident.

'What kind of an accident?' barks the attendant.

# Pop and Me

My dad had come along to watch me,
the day I came last in the cub scout sack race;
the day my glasses fell off on to the running track
and somebody behind me
deliberately hopped on top of them,
damaging them really badly.
I was that struggling runt at the back,
laughed at by everyone –
everyone except my dad.
And not because he had
a beating in mind,
but because he felt for me.
And when he came to find me
and I was melting with tears,
he said 'You're the one
they'll remember in the years to come, son.
You were very funny.'
And he took me to the shop
and ordered me some pop,
and we halved the humiliation
when he didn't have the money.

# The Halo and the Dozy Dozen

The Lord was born without sin
but not without his thin flat halo.
The wise men they were reverent,
the shepherds they were coarser:
'That shiny, floating hat,' said one,
'it's like a flying saucer.'

In his last years,
the Lord would regularly cast his halo
into the wilderness
as part of his dog's exercise regime,
and he once tried to amuse his disciples
by holding it like a steering wheel.
'What is it, boys, a bus or a car?'
'But we don't know what buses or cars are, Lord,'
answered his bewildered team,
and the Lord set his dog unto them.

# These Were Your Father's

(1994)

# A Few Words about Poetry

Adrian Mitchell suggested that most people ignore most poetry because most poetry ignores most people, to which I would add that most porcupines ignore most putty because putty is usually quite high off the ground and porcupines usually aren't, and they tend not to notice things unless they're of an edible, threatening or sexually attractive nature.

D.H. Lawrence spoke of poetry as that which brings a new attention to something. This is what the Martian poets were after; Craig Raine, through his Martian eye, sees the book as a many-winged bird. Similarly, a pair of glasses might be seen as a bird with no wings, no body, no head and a pair of glasses.

## Holy Orders

Be sharp, be blunt,
hunt out the fox
of your own vox popular.
Be jocular, be ocular,
however much they mocular;
be rigorous, irregular,
but don't go being negular.
Whip away the regular
from being smugly smugular.
When going for the jugular,
refrain from being ugular:
enlighten and surprise,
put a sparkle in their eyes
and a few quid in your pocket.

# Brother Trevor

He handed in his cowl
and his trowel
and took leave of his order for ever,
taking a position as a warder
in an already overcrowded prison.
After the celibate years,
being thought of as 'a screw'
took a bit of getting used to,
and in spite of having no cell of his own now,
he found the new uniform didn't allow
quite as much freedom of movement.

# The Cub Scout Diary

One Christmas I told my dad
that my sister had scribbled on the pages of my new cub scout diary.
When he confronted her about the damage
and she pleaded innocent,
I asked who did it if she hadn't,
and realising there was no other likely suspect,
assuming our parents to be above such a senseless violation,
Angela said that although she had no
recollection of the incident,
the culprit must have been her;
an admission which my father felt
warranted a thorough beating.
What had actually occurred was,
whilst entering my address in the diary,
which I wanted to look as neat as possible,
I had made a mistake,
crossed it out, made a mess
and lost my temper,
ruining the book
with a series of indelible markings.
When the frenzy was over,
I decided that somebody should suffer for this act of destruction
and that person should be my sister.

# Money Well Spent

He knew he'd been done but he'd had to have it; he loved anything old to do with scouting, and this book of camping hints was a real find and the stallholder knew it. Thirty quid! But he'd had the money and what was he getting for it? Beauty, antiquity; you couldn't put a price on that. The date, nineteen twenty-eight; they knew nothing of a Second World War then. The book was a beautiful orange and not at all faded at the edges. The staples too were in fine condition, no additional rust-orange against the inner whiteness of the pages; but thirty quid was still steep.

There were plenty of the old adverts which he loved, because the things which they publicised were things you could no longer buy. The addresses, if they still existed, would have gone through many incarnations since the time of publication, yet the text knew nothing of this and innocently promised the advertised goods for a very reasonable and archaic remittance.

He turned to the first page of the scouting material. Why was it he was so fascinated by scouting? He read a résumé of the Scout law: 'Trusty, loyal and helpful, brotherly, courteous, kind, obedient, smiling and thrifty, and clean in thought, word and mind.' He did not agree that all the properties listed were qualities, but it was the attempt at a code for right living that attracted him, and it was something the modern world disowned – well, he didn't. The Boy Scout movement might be moving towards obsolescence but the founding concept was sound enough. There was much good amongst the nonsense: the fetching hats, the wacky salute, the knotting, the yarns, the alertness; he loved it as a boy, he loved it still.

He smelled the book and, as he did so, he sniffed up the molecules of another age and went into a deep deep reverie like a campfire sleep. He was taken back to a scout hut somewhere in the nineteen-twenties. The book was new, and now it had returned to its own time and it had taken its loyal reader with it. The group of scouts in the middle of whom he had landed were rather surprised, but their skipper had always realised that the circles and rituals were a potent invocation, and John set about trying to do good scout work to challenge the course of history, and the troop became his helpers, and John had no doubt in his mind that the book had been worth thirty quid.

# Friendship

On this ship of friends,
if your heart sank
I would gladly walk the plank
and dive five fathoms
into your sea of troubles.


## Deep in Shallow Waters

Relieving myself in the Mediterranean,
it occurs to me that some of my wee
has become part of the wider sea,
which triggers thoughts of individuals
who think they're really big
when really they are piddly.

## *Res Romanae* (Roman Things)

When we were sat in Latin,
the teacher used to very occasionally break the tension
of verb and noun declension
by getting us to get out
our *Res Romanae* books for ten minutes or so.
These were little books in which we registered
the Roman proverb and the Roman pun,
the things the Romans did for fun,
like swimming
and skimming flattish pebbles
discus-like across the sea.
Still pretty dull,
but we got by
a little better
with *Res Romanae* – Roman things.

On the long last day of a summer term,
the heat indoors made the pupils squirm,
and the teacher, who was very firm,
softened up for once and said
'Today we shall do something different.'
And eagerly we started chattin',
imagining some cricket battin' –
a pleasure he would deny.
'For the WHOLE lesson, boys,' he told us,
'we shall enjoy our *Res Romanae*.'

# On Hadrian's Wall

I imagined local children had a bladder just for kicks;
I could see them booting their ball about,
down the centuries
and up against the bricks.


# Wheelchairs in Ancient Rome

Did they lack appropriate access?
Did the stacked steps
consistently cause despair?
Not if yours was the Emperor's wheelchair!


# No Credit

The pyramids are a wonder,
but we're left to wonder who
the brickies were who did the job;
there must have been a few
of them, mustn't there?

And the Bible names the wiseguys
with the frankincense and myrrh,
but who knows who the shepherds were?

They didn't get a credit.
They got lost in the edit.

# Hospital Art

In the afternoons, between toileting
the doubly-incontinent patients
and giving them their tea,
there were a couple of hours
in which the staff and patients usually sat around staring into space.
I might have been the same after a few years in the place,
but being an enthusiastic newcomer
and a student on vacation,
I said 'Hey, let's get everybody doing art!'
So I got the materials we needed,
sat everyone around tables and proceeded.
They were not the most capable of artists
but together we made some things which, put up on the wall together,
really brightened up the ward.
The next day I was not working
and on my return I found the walls to be bare.
The staff nurse had torn down the pictures:
he told me they were ugly
and they underlined the inabilities of the patients.
I said that the pictures had gone
because they were a reminder
of the fact that he spent the afternoons staring into space
rather than trying to do something creative
with those in his care.
I said he was a disgrace.
I said I hope you're very proud,
but I didn't say it aloud.

# My Father's Pullover

My father was older than other dads
and when I was fifteen or so
I used to call him 'old man'.
When I was younger, such abuse
would have triggered prolific use
of the back of his hand,
but I think he thought me too old and too big for that now,
not that he was cowardly;
I got the feeling that he was prepared
to square up to any aggressor,
but a full-scale physical to-do with his adolescent son
would have given him a sense of parental failure.
I remember that in his frustration with my insolence
he would involuntarily pull down the bottom of his sleeveless pullover,
which I would imitate
to make his frustration greater.

# The Weekender

I once went on what was called a Weekender, in a hotel up in Grange-over-Sands. I'd seen them advertised when I was doing a show in the area. I took a train up there. It was at the very beginning of the mobile phone boom, and for the whole journey there were three separate people on and off these infernal machines – and that was just at my table. To be truthful, when I say the whole journey I only mean the InterCity part from London to Lancaster. At Lancaster I had to change to a local train, on which I was accompanied by two of the mobile maniacs, whom I avoided by parking myself in a separate compartment where electronic game machines seemed to be the thing.

I object to mobile phones on trains because they are an imposition of something private in a public area, usually by people who'd kick up a right old stink if the transgression was the other way round.

Arriving in Grange-over-Sands, I popped down into the town to get myself some condoms 'just in case', then made my way up the hill to the hotel. In the foyer there was a huge dog, a Great Dane I think, which moved about with difficulty. The person at the reception desk spoke familiarly with the dog and had an intriguing toupée. After receiving my key and Weekender welcome letter, I took my duffle bags up the grand Victorian staircase to my room, number one-ten. To my delight I was at the front of the hotel, with a wonderful view of the gardens and greenery beyond. To my dismay I discovered rather a lot of dog muck in the bathroom. After reporting my discovery, I was apologetically moved to the room next door, number one-eleven, which had an equally enchanting view, but from a slightly different angle. I settled down to enjoy my welcoming letter. 'Dear Guest,' it began disappointingly, but then the text went on less formally, inviting me for drinks with all the other guests at 6.30 p.m. Great, I thought, that's in half an hour from now.

After a quick sort-out and shower, I made my way down the grand old Victorian staircase to face my fellow Weekenders. I was to discover that they were all at the senior citizen end of the age spectrum, apart from two young people jabbering into their mobiles, whom I decided to ignore, introducing myself instead to a lively older woman who was talking to the hotel dog.

We got chattering and I discovered that she shared my interest in railway travel and the television programme *Blockbusters*. Our conversation was curtailed when she went up to bed at eight o'clock, but not before we had agreed to take the train to Barrow-in-Furness the following morning. For the remainder of the evening I chatted with the dog.

Upstairs, I mixed up my complimentary cup of cocoa and relaxed reflectively in my complimentary armchair. It hadn't been the best birthday I'd had, but it certainly wasn't the worst. It was certainly the second worst, though, I argued with myself. 'Stop your moaning and turn on the telly.' I did as I was ordered and suddenly I perked up; they were advertising a new programme called *Bob's Your Uncle* and, for a moment, I thought this referred to Bob Holness, the quizmaster in *Blockbusters*, but it didn't.

The night saw a tall fall of snow, which considerably increased my relish for the next day's outing. Dora, understandably, greeted the sight of the white with less enthusiasm, on account of her greater brittleness of bone. We made our way down to the station, however, without mishap, and happily sat reading our respective morning papers as we awaited the ten o'clock from Preston. I said to Dora that it was a very good sign if people felt relaxed enough to sit reading things together, and Dora said she'd appreciate it if I didn't interrupt her while she was reading, and she'd prefer it if I called her Mrs Phelps. She didn't speak to me again until we were arriving in Barrow, and that was only to ask me to swap papers. Fortunately there was nothing in mine which took her fancy and we had a comprehensive look around the shops, a long leisurely sit in the caff with some books we'd purchased, and a gorgeous journey back in the twilight snow, marred only by a couple of interruptions from Mrs Phelps' mobile phone.

*To be continued...*

# Bus Conduct

After an undignified boarding
with his can of Special Strength,
the old inebriate staggered half the length
of the crowded lower deck,
then levelled a dishevelled request
at a tidier young woman
to provide him with a seat.
Uncomplaining, she complied,
the sign said to give it up to the elderly,
and social disadvantages aside,
this man qualified.
And after a slightly unsettling period of settling in,
he was able to get on
with the business of belligerence
to persons unspecified,
in relative comfort.

# The Lord's Dog

She could jump as high as heaven.
She was the sheep dog the shepherds gave him
to help him save his flock,
the one he kept alive for thirty-three years
on one tin of God food.
You hear about the preaching and praying
but not about the Lord saying
'Good dog, there's a good dog.'
Nor about all the tricks he taught her:
'Walkies, walkies on water.'
Nor about the way she barked at Pontius Pilate
and marked her master's loss
by marking out her territory
up against the cross
apostle.

## A Trip to the Theatre

As I rambled over the ruined stage
of the Roman arena,
imagining the sword-bearing audience
of another age,
someone whose clothes look cleaner
than mine, who must have seen
a sign that I had not,
got somewhat
unreasonable:
'Could you keep to the paths, please,
you're setting a bad example to my son!'
Politely I explained the innocence of my misdemeanour,
but inside,
my slighted pride
imagined how I might have been obscener
or, better still, obscurer:
'Madam, under this world's wondrous dome,
I walk where I want to,
for I am a citizen of ancient Rome!'

# The Weekender *continued*

Saturday evening was designated in our Weekender's programme as a games evening, and Mr Desk, the hotel manager, came into the lounge with a pile of board games which he placed on the table saying, 'Help yourselves, everybody. Be my guests.'

Mrs Phelps and I opted for draughts, and we had thirty games in all, all of which I won, although in no way did this detract from my partner's enjoyment. 'It's not the winning that counts, it's the contact with the wood,' she said, keeling over onto the parquet flooring.

After a reviving cup of tea, I suggested that perhaps she might like to retire. 'Yes, I think I would,' she answered, 'and perhaps you might like to join me in church tomorrow morning?'

'Which church would that be?'

'The Church of Christ the Martian.'

'I don't believe I'm familiar with that one?'

'I'm the only member.'

'But where's the actual church?'

'It's in my heart.'

'How will I accompany you?'

'I'll set up a couple of candles in my room, if you like.'

'What kind of service will it be, though?'

'Room service,' said Mrs Phelps, for the first time allowing her comedic facility into our acquaintance.

In the chapel of room 107, the next morning, Mrs Phelps explained her denomination's thoughts on the Son of God.

'Well, originally he came down from Mars as a dog. Mary didn't give birth to him, though, she caught him as he fell out of the spaceship and then put him in the manger, the same as it says in the Bible. Then one of the wise men gave him a pair of glasses which made him human...'

'It sounds rather far fetched to me.'

'Yes, but not as far fetched as it sounds to people who knock on your door wanting to talk about religion.'

After the room service we embarked upon a snowy woodland walk, during which I collected some bits for my contribution to the Weekender Fancy Dress Finale which I'd seen advertised in the hotel foyer.

Back in the warmth of the lounge I began to sew my costume and Mrs Phelps got on with some needlework of her own as we conversed in that slightly detached way that you might do in a primary school art lesson.

'But don't you think mobile phones and computers are a sign of progress?'

'Well, in a way I do, but really I think it's progress in the wrong direction.'

'Do you really?'

'Mm. I mean there's more human interaction in a game of hop-scotch than in a computer game.'

'That's true, but there's more chalk isn't there?'

'Yes... What do you mean?' I said, half coming out of my reverie.

'Chalk makes a mess of the pavement, doesn't it?'

'Oh, right, but not of society. I think mobile phones and computer games and all that stuff isolate people; they're not really progress at all, they increase the sense of self but not the sense of community.'

'What about the sense of humour?'

'I think you'd better leave the jokes to me, Mrs Phelps. What do you think of these sleeves made of leaves I've made?'

'Very nice, John.'

That evening, when I knocked on her door to go down to the party, Mrs Phelps appeared with a smile and a slice of cucumber which she described to me as Martian holy communion.

'I'm nearly ready; and I won't be needing these,' she said, taking off her spectacles and turning into a dog.

My own costume was what I described as a bloke-tree; it consisted of the leaves I'd sewn onto my shirt and plenty of brown paper, wrapped tightly about my legs. Soon I was hopping happily down the Grand Hotel staircase, preceded by the excited yaps and yelps of Mrs Phelps, although apparently the notice I'd seen in the foyer was out of date and there was no fancy dress party scheduled for that evening.

# Five Sugars Please

(1993)

## Glasses Good, Contact Lenses Bad

In the embrace of my glasses,
I openly accept my vulnerability
and affirm my acceptance of outside help.
As well as providing open acknowledgment
of the imperfection in my eyesight,
my glasses are a symbolic celebration
of the wider imperfection that is the human condition.
In contrast, contact lenses are a hiding of the fault;
they pretend the self-sufficiency of the individual
and minister unto the cult of stultifying normality.
They are that which should be cast out of your vision:
they are a denial of the self,
they are a denial of the other,
they are a betrayal of humanity.

# The Difference between Truth and Adequacy

Our Nature of Scientific Activity tutor explained
that with scientific theories
near is
sometimes close enough.
He gave the example of a law
of which science had been sure,
which had been obeyed
unquestioningly since it was made,
but which was later discovered to ignore
certain variables;
sometimes what is seen as objective fact
is in fact only a rough guide,
which does the job of ordering
rather than describing reality.
Applying this idea
to what is printed here,
adequacy might say
'It's there in black and white.'
Whereas I think the truth would rather cite
two shades of grey
of which one's extremely light.

# The Difference between Dogs and Sheds

It's not a very good idea to give a dog
a coat
of creosote.

# French Letters – English Words

I'd like to commission a poem about condoms, she said.
I'll see what I can come up with, I jested.
And I considered the phrase 'electronically tested',
and imagined the poor little things
shot through with voltage and pain,
and thought of starting a campaign
to stop it.
And I thought about the campaign
to tell penis-users they might cop it
without one – a condom not a penis, that is.
Protection and collection
in those little rubber teats
is something that can save your life
and also save your sheets.

# A Short Address at the Comedy College

I hope
you will beware of putting comedy
under the microscope.
To dissect it,
first you must kill it,
you must lose the thrill, chill it.
I don't wish my fish
to be a fillet.
Would you beach a whale
merely for teaching porpoises?
I don't want to appear
on a graph,
and I don't want to dread
what comes after
the laughter's dead.
And that's it, I said.
And as I was leaving the class,
I fell on my arse.

# Greed

Once, when I wanted my sister's sweets,
I pretended to be a hungry dog,
and each time she dropped one on the floor,
I amused her with my comical scavenging.
And when all her sweets had gone,
I stopped and got on with my own,
taking no interest in the hungry dog
that looked very much like my sister.

# Can I Come Down Now, Dad?

(1991)

## Forever Roman

Mile after Roman mile,
travelling from Newcastle to Carlisle,
in spite of seeing Hadrian's Wall
now fallen like the empire,
I imagined a Roman at that empire's height,
standing by the roadside
and seeing the way of the Romans
stretching to a distance
as far as this moment of mine.
A Roman with a future,
for whom the sun was equally high
under an identical blue sky.

## Sat on the Pillar of Hercules

I bought a book about Roman eroticism,
with images and artefacts
the museums had banned.
Just for research purposes, you'll understand.

## The Pillars of the Gods

In the dark ages,
the remains of Roman extravagance
must have been a topmost mystery
to a population with such a lack
of building skills
and history teachers.
Who were these beings
with such a miraculous knack
of stacking stones?
Where did they go?
And, more unnervingly,
when would they be back?

## Digging for It

Sometimes a poem is less of an invention
and more of a find.
Its birth a kind
of archaeology,
a job of unearthing and piecing together,
and sometimes a piece won't fit
because it's part of something else,
and sometimes it is just a bit of old rubbish.

## These National Health Glasses

These National Health Glasses were devised
before the vision of the people got privatised.

## Pat

I said Pat,
you are fat,
and you are cataclysmically desirable.
And to think I used to think
that slim was where it's at.
Well, not any more, Pat.
You've changed that.
You love yourself,
you flatter yourself,
you shatter their narrow image of the erotic.
And Pat said,
'What do you mean FAT?'

## On Hampstead Heath

I ask you what sort of tree
we are sat underneath
and you tell me it is a big one.
You ask me how I came by the scar on my knee
and I tell you I hurt myself once.
A passer-by, possibly Austrian
and possibly a Christian,
points to a fluorescent cycle clip in the grass
and wonders if I might have lost it.
I stand up and indicate that I am wearing shorts.

# The Stand-up Comedian Sits Down

The comedian climbs onto the stage
and truthfully points out
that the microphone smells of sick.
So does your breath, says somebody.
Get on with it, says somebody else.
Please settle down,
replies the comedian, responding well.
I'll start this routine if it kills me.
There is an outbreak of cheering
at the mention of his death.
Get off, says the one who said get on with it,
and the comedian comes up with a line
so apt and incisive
that any further heckling is redundant.
Unfortunately, he comes up with it
on the bus home.

# The Brother-in-Law
# and Other Animals

(1986)

## His Heart's in the Wrong Place, It Should Be in the Glove Compartment

After his favourite vegetarian meal,
consisting of seventeen pints of lager,
my brother-in-law offers me a lift home.
On the way, we stop off for a drink.
At the bar, I ask for two halves of lager.
My brother-in-law says there is no such thing as a half of lager.
I suggest we get the bus the rest of the way.
My brother-in-law says that buses are only for scum
and that if he comes in his car,
he leaves in his car.
Before we leave and discover that his car has been stolen,
my brother-in-law tells me
how he likes to stop and ask hitch-hikers where they are going
and then tell them that he will get there first.

# I Wouldn't Say My Brother-in-Law Was Fat, Because He Is Quite Thin

He's as miserable as sin
but not as interesting.
He's as open as the pub is at twenty past four
in the morning,
and as welcome as an open sore
on your eye,
but he thinks he's great.
He isn't beautiful,
he's horrible.
He eats crisps in the cinema as a matter of principle.
In a previous incarnation he was a beer crate.
If he does you a favour then you know that you're in debt.
If you want someone to help you, he's a very outside bet.
If you were in a lifeboat and someone had to go
and my brother-in-law was there,
you wouldn't exactly need a ballot.
He's ten stone in his pyjamas
and that's ten stone overweight.
He's not exactly an artist
but they should hang him in the Tate.
He was an adult from the age of eight,
and whatever age he dies at it will be far too late.
I don't like him.

## His Heart's in the Wrong Place, It Should Be in the Dustbin

The other night I went to see my brother-in-law for a chat.
After five minutes he went and sat in the garage.
After ten minutes he came back in saying
Here, John, are you staying the night?
If that's all right, I said.
Then he was gone,
up to the spare bedroom
to change the sheets,
to put the dirty ones back on.

## Christmas with the Brother-in-Law (Oh what fun)

The two clip-on earrings slip from our Christmas cracker.
You can have them, John,
my brother-in-law quips.
I slip into the earrings.
How do I look then, handsome? I lie to him.
All right, John, very sexy. Take them off, he says,
trying to sound normal in his torn Christmas hat
that is sat around his neck.
You're not a woman, he reminds me.
How do you explain these, then? I reply,
ripping open my shirt and squirting my nipples at him.
Shall I take these off, too?
Don't spoil the Christmas, John, my mother interrupts.

## Sister

Sister, you are an alchemist.
Base metals into gold you cannot do.
But I have seen you
turn boredom into joy
and make toys from the rubbish.
Sister you are an alchemist.
But you have not done a very good job
with your husband.

# The Imagination

The only nation worth defending.
A nation without alienation.
A nation whose flag is invisible
and whose borders are forever beyond the horizon.
A nation whose motto is 'Why have one or the other
when you can have one, the other and both.'
A nation whose badge is a chrysanthemum of sweet-wrappings,
maybe.
A nation whose laws are magnificent,
whose customs are not barriers,
whose uniform is multiform,
whose anthem is improvised,
whose hour is imminent
and whose leader is me.

# A Dog and a Pigeon

In a shocking flurry of feathers,
a seemingly pleasant dog attacked a pigeon in the park.
The badly-shaken owner tethered the attacker,
who began to bark.
If that dog can kill, I said,
you should let it finish the job.
No, said another witness,
it's not our job to interfere with nature.
The owner looked.
The pigeon bled.
It's your dog – your decision, I said.
I'll let him go, said the owner,
and then it's up to Fred.
So Fred is freed
and the bleeding bird
is shaken and left, but still not dead.
It's even worse now, the owner whimpers.
A brick on the head, then, I say.
I can't, says the owner, beginning to weep.
Can you – can you do it?
Then my brother-in-law comes over
with half a paving stone.
I'll do it, he says,
for ten quid.

# In a Boat in Plymouth Harbour

About to embark
on a tour of the bay,
we pay our one-pound-fifties
and we're off.
*Good morning, Ladies and Gentlemen.*
*Here we are at the mouth of the Tamar.*
*To your right is Devon and on your left is Cornwall.*
Now, that's interesting.
I'd forgotten how the river forms a natural boundary
between the two counties.
I remember old Taffy Bennett telling us that in geography.
Well, that's twenty-five-pence worth already.
*And on your right again is a statue of King William of Orange.*
Mmm – just how I'd imagined him,
only bigger.
*And up ahead, there you can see a nuclear submarine.*
Oh dear.
I do hope we don't have a war.
I wave to a man working on the deck of the sub
but he does not wave back.
It is my brother-in-law.

FROM

# Visions of the Bone Idol

(1984)

# Max

*(likes to be with people but people don't like to be with Max)*

Max is a dog with a problem.
The sort of problem it's a job to ignore.
The first time they all thought it was funny,
but not any more.
Picture the scene. This home-loving hound
is sleeping by the fire with the family round.
He wakes up and makes a little sound.
Little Albert gets it first,
he's nearest the ground.
Albert's mum gets wind of it
and she say open the door.
And whatever we've been feeding him,
I don't think we should give him no more.
Max does another one, like old kippers,
wakes up daddy in his fireside slippers.
Daddy wakes up and says, open the door.
Albert says, it's open dad, I did it when he did it before.
Then mum says, it's hard to relax with Max about.
Yesterday it happened while we were out in the car.
And it's a small car.
And granny, she was sick.
She's not used to it like we are.
Maybe we should swap him for a budgerigar.
Max is smelly,
he can spoil your telly.
But luckily
he's not and elephant.

## Grandad's Glasses

We never used to ask questions
about his glasses.
He needed them to see the telly
and that was that.
But then one day
he couldn't see the telly anymore,
so he didn't need his glasses.
What were we to do?
It seemed wrong to throw away the glasses
but there was no point in burying them with him
because
    a) His eyes were shut, and
    b) None of us believed in telly after death.
We had a family get together about it,
and after the big argument
we came up with two possibilities
    a) Find someone with glasses like grandad's
and give them the glasses, and
    b) Find someone with glasses like grandad's
and sell them the glasses.

# Index of titles